SILVERSTONE AND FORMULA 1

ANTHONY MEREDITH & GORDON BLACKWELL

AMBERLEY

Above: Formula 1 in 1956: The International Trophy. *Left-right*: Stirling Moss (Vanwall), Harry Schell (Vanwall), Juan Manuel Fangio (Lancia) and Mike Hawthorn (BRM) head off from the front row.

First published 2022

Amberley Publishing
The Hill, Stroud,
Gloucestershire, GL5 4EP

www.amberley-books.com

ISBN: 978 1 3981 0484 6 (print)
ISBN: 978 1 3981 0485 3 (ebook)

British Library Cataloguing in Publication Data.
A catalogue record for this book is available from the British Library.

Typeset in 10pt on 12pt Celeste.
Typesetting by SJmagic DESIGN SERVICES, India.
Printed in the UK.

GLAMOROUS GARDEN PARTIES

A PERSONAL INTRODUCTION

A few years ago, that knowledgeable Silverstone legend Gordon Blackwell helped me put together an account of how the former wartime airfield turned itself into a famous motor racing venue. *Silverstone Circuit Through Time* was shortly afterwards followed by *Silverstone's First Grand Prix, 1948*, our in-depth look at the very first race meeting held there.

Silverstone and Formula 1 carries on from where the British GP of 1948 left off, exploring the all-important relationship between the circuit and motor sport's elite formula. Few would disagree that it has been this association that has most helped bring the former airfield its worldwide fame. From the very first, the pizzazz surrounding Formula 1 attracted great crowds. The RAF's unwanted ugly duckling suddenly found itself transformed into a glamorous entertainment centre, and the glamour of Silverstone and Formula 1 has mesmerised each succeeding generation. As the bearded Delphic Oracle of *Motor Sport* Denis Jenkinson once famously put it, every time the circus descends on Silverstone, 'a great and glorious summer garden party ensues'. This atmosphere still obtains, even though in recent years the circuit has been experiencing a major make-over, a metamorphosis into an impressively high-tech and super-de-luxe centre of motor sport. Indeed, as Silverstone welcomes the annual arrival of the Formula 1 circus, its setting is now even more glamorous than ever. Great and glorious summer garden parties live on.

The circuit and the racing formula's twin destinies seem always to have been linked. They have grown up together. It was in 1947 that the long-established governing body of motor sport, the Fédération Internationale de l'Automobile, deemed that the leading single-seater category would be called Formula 1. A year later, the FIA announced a Formula 1 Drivers' World Championship, starting in 1950 with Silverstone hosting the first of its seven rounds. Formula 1, then, officially began that year, but it would seem churlish to ignore the circuit's important formative years of 1948–49.

That so many great drivers were to ply their skills around the circuit led us to some hard editorial decisions. Whom should we include? Whom should we reluctantly leave out? Our choices have veered towards the home-bred, but perhaps with good justification. British drivers, engineers and entrepreneurs have long played a central part in Formula 1, and Silverstone has always been a place for Union Jacks. Since 1952, too, the circuit has been under the care of the British Racing Drivers' Club. The Club's current President, David Coulthard, twice won the British Grand Prix. His predecessors include Derek Warwick, Damon Hill and Jackie Stewart. British Racing Green may be largely a thing of the past, but the BRDC's committee and 800 members are still imbued with that inspirational colour and doing their very best to ensure the continuance of the Formula 1 summer garden party.

It is a party that inspires reminiscences of past excitements and, in particular, those times when we all first began to participate. Gordon Blackwell, for example, as a very young boy living nearby in Dadford, was taken by his parents as early as 1949. 'We locals, of course, knew a route through the woods that brought us to Stowe Corner. There were no fences in those distant days. No men at the gate. So there used to be quite a friendly local gathering down between Stowe and Club! Being small, I would usually be allowed to watch from the very front.' Two images in particular remain with him from the Grand Prix of 1949. 'We were watching from Club and I was mesmerised by the magnificent bright yellow Talbot-Lago of Johnny Claes, clearly on the limit. He would disappear from view in a dip after Club and reappear in the distance as he approached Abbey. I can still see and hear, too, a local ambulance clanking its bell as it slowly made its way down the slope from Stowe. John Bolster had had a bad crash. A sombre reminder of the dangers involved, particularly in those early days.' Sometimes, on the occasions when Gordon couldn't squeeze to the front of the crowd, his father would find a tree on which to hoist him. 'It was marvellous! I shall always remember watching from a tree as the great Argentinian Gonzales came speeding down Hangar Straight and spun at Stowe.'

Silverstone was not unusual in the perfunctory measures taken in those times for the safety of both drivers and spectators. Miraculously, there was no tragic accident involving the crowd. Gordon remembers one club race in 1955 when a wheel detached itself from an errant machine and looped up into the air. 'I was watching with a friend in the very basic, roof-less stand at Woodcote. The wheel made quite a noise and left quite a mark on the wooden flooring as it came down right behind us! Its flight was later captured by a photo in *Autosport!*'

My own first visit, somewhat later than Gordon's, was in 1963. I'd just discovered the excitement of a Goodwood club meeting and resolved to try a Grand Prix. Having driven up from the south coast, hood down in my newly acquired, long-bonneted and somewhat ancient Allard, I parked in Buckingham marketplace. Someone had confidently assured me that I could walk from there. That confidence proved disastrously misplaced, but I did eventually reach the circuit, on the back of some kind person's motorbike, just in time for the eighty-two laps of the Grand Prix.

The year 1963 belonged to a strangely low-powered formula, but the sight and sound of the entire pack, all twenty-three of them, emerging together from Chapel Curve to tear down towards Stowe, was absolutely thrilling. History relates that two Brabhams were in front (Dan Gurney on the heels of Jack), with pole-sitter Jim Clark back in the pack. It wasn't too long, however, before Clark was leading in his tiny Lotus of British Racing Green. Only John Surtees and Graham Hill were on the same lap by the end, but interest never wavered. Partly it was the slim-lined cars, teetering on the brink of adhesion as they drifted dramatically round Stowe. Partly, the star names. Partly, too, the summer garden party atmosphere. They raced for well over two hours but it was over far too soon.

Several hours later, the long-bonneted Allard was speeding south, pretending for a while to be a Lotus 25. Alas, I was unable in my impecunious state to assuage for ever its constant thirst (10 miles a gallon). It was shortly sold for £50. Jim Clark's great victory of 1963 had been its swansong.

Anthony Meredith

THE GRAND PRIX AND INTERNATIONAL TROPHY
1948-49

There had been two British Grand Prix at Brooklands in the 1920s and four at Donington Park in the 1930s, but neither circuit was available when the RAC decided to celebrate the end of the Second World War by reviving the event. The RAC accordingly turned to the old wartime airfield of Silverstone. It was to prove a key moment in the history of British motor sport.

The British Grand Prix of 1948 proved such a success that in 1949 the idea was hatched to have two visits from the Grand Prix cars: in May for the RAC's Grand Prix and in August for a second race, sponsorship for which would be needed. 'If motor racing is to become a popular sport in this country,' wrote *Motor Sport*'s Bill Boddy at this time, 'it must have the backing of one of the great national newspapers.' Max Aitken, Lord Beaverbrook's sports-minded son, recently decorated in the war for his bravery and skill as a fighter pilot, answered the call. The *Daily Express* came forward to sponsor the second Formula 1 race, the International Trophy. It was to become a really popular annual event in its own right. Happily, too, when Silverstone had to alternate with Aintree (1955–62) and Brands Hatch (1964–86) as the venue for the British Grand Prix, it could still host Formula 1 through the *Daily Express* International Trophy.

A snapshot of Club Corner during the Grand Prix of 1949. The straw bales of the one-off Club chicane are just visible on the left. Far away: the hangars on Hangar Straight.

The Strangely Sited Paddock and Pits, 1948–51

Luigi Villoresi climbs from his winning Maserati during a 1948 Grand Prix pit stop. This recently discovered snapshot shows the roof of a farm building behind the pits, a big feature of the first paddock. The start line (between Abbey and Woodcote) was immediately behind the bridge just visible to the right of the spectators' heads. *Below*: The main entrance gate (19) today, with the roof of the extant farm building to be seen directly behind the F1 noticeboard.

The Hastily Improvised Pits, 1948

An early morning snapshot of the French Lago-Talbot team cars awaiting action. Above the *Autocar* advert, a Dunlop van can just be seen in the paddock; so, too, the silhouette of a distant hangar. *Below*: A little later on in the day, Alberto Ascari relaxes in his Maserati 4CLT (11). The 4CLT's elderly engine derived its awesome power from twin superchargers. Meanwhile, John Bolster's B-type ERA (25) and David Hampshire's A-type ERA (24) receive attention. The farm building in the paddock looms large.

The Maserati 4CLT, Then and Now

Prince Bira of Siam exits Maggots in the 1948 Grand Prix (a 90-degree corner that year, approached from a runway) in his brand-new Maserati 4CLT. He came fifth. *Below*: Two gloriously restored 4CLTs on display at Silverstone in 2018: the famous car that Fangio took to victory several times, in Argentina's yellow and blue, and the red 4CLT that Reg Parnell drove in the 1948 Grand Prix, now on permanent display in the Museo Ferrari, Modena. In the background a taller, slower and distinctly more elderly ERA.

The ERA's Good-looking E-type

Peter Walker at the wheel of GP1, the first ERA E-type, in the 1949 International Trophy, with the Stowe grandstands on the horizon as he speeds away from Club towards Abbey. ERA's post-war owner, Leslie Johnson, had briefly impressed with this same car in the 1948 GP. *Below*: GP1, completely rebuilt, most successfully raced by Duncan Ricketts and on display (behind the Wing) in the circuit's 70th anniversary celebration. Beyond are Geoff Richardson's ERA-Riley and Lord Selsdon's elderly Talbot, both present at Silverstone at its historic first ever meeting.

The New and Not-so-new, 1949

'Gigi' Villoresi in Ferrari's first Formula 1 car (the Ferrari 125 with a supercharged 1.5 litre V12 engine) at Club Corner during the International Trophy of 1949. Villoresi's similarly equipped teammate, Alberto Ascari, won the race. *Below*: Louis Chiron (Lago Talbot) in the same event. Derived from the 1930s, the French Lago-Talbots (with unsupercharged 4.5 litre engines), though still important participants in 1948–49 and magnificent in the French national colours of light blue, were severely outpaced by those in flaming red.

2

FORZA, ALFA! FORZA, FERRARI!
1950-51

The new World Championship fired national spirit and ensured the appearance of the Alfa Romeo team. Although their superb Tipo 158 'Alfettas' dated back to 1939, with the latest power increase from their two-stage superchargers they could reach 180 mph. A quarrel over starting money had meant their non-appearance in 1948 and, with the loss of three drivers, they had retired from the 1949 season. Now, in 1950, with Fangio, Farina and Fagioli vying for team leadership, Alfa Romeo were back in a big way. Dr Giuseppe 'Nino' Farina would win both Silverstone races as well as the first Drivers' World Championship.

Meanwhile, in England, the personable Raymond Mays was drumming up wide support for his ambitious venture, a world-beating BRM with intricate 16-cylinder engine. Its first appearance, at the 1950 GP, disappointed – just a few careful demonstration laps. Worse followed. At the start of the International Trophy the BRM dramatically expired. Although two finished in the 1951 GP, Reg Parnell suffered a nightmare: 'My leg was badly burnt and my right hand a mass of blisters. I hardly knew what was happening at the chequered flag. I staggered to the first-aid tent. The cockpit must have ventilation! The seat must fit each driver! The wheels are apt to flap on corners – the road-holding needs adjustment!'

A private Ferrari (Peter Whitehead) versus a works Alfa Romeo (Farina) at the 1950 International Trophy. A hangar looms behind the stands. People line the track ... (BRDC)

The Superb Alfettas

Fangio leads his teammate Farina through Chapel in the 1950 GP. The shrewd Fangio, who had arrived in Europe in 1949 with several other Argentinian drivers, two Maserati 4CLTs and the support of his country's dictator, General Peron, had moved to Alfa mid-season 1950. *Below* (BRDC): Forty-three-year-old 'Nino' Farina (a former cavalry officer with a doctorate from Turin University) leads fifty-one-year-old Luigi Fagioli round Stowe later in the same race. Fagioli, the only F1 winner born in the 1800s, perished two years later.

A Glimpse of Past Glory

A recent star exhibit at Silverstone: a Tipo 179 Alfetta, kindly loaned by the Alfa Romeo Museo Storico of Arese, Milan, to commemorate Farina's triumph of 1950. Though of very similar appearance to Farina's Tipo 178, in fact the Tipo 179 had an upgraded engine, brakes and transmission. It was to take Fangio to his first World Championship in 1951. Alas, in 1952 a shortage of F1 machinery led to a dramatic change in the regulations, and the glorious Alfettas were seen no more.

Setting the Pace

For the 1950 Grand Prix, the three works drivers were joined by thirty-nine-year-old Reg Parnell (above), the leading British driver of the post-war era, in a fourth Alfetta. Streetwise and mechanically well-informed, Parnell was determined to be given equal equipment. He wasn't, but still finished an admirable third. *Below*: 'Nino' Farina, speeding away at Abbey on his majestic way to winning the 1950 International Trophy. To his right are the farm (hidden by trees) and the old airfield's control tower. (Photos: BRDC)

Making-up Numbers

Two ERAs approaching Stowe in the 1950 GP. Cuth Harrison (modified type B) and Leslie Johnson (frail type E) were typical of the many enthusiastic participants who had uncompetitive machinery. Johnson's ERA, alas, would catch fire after two laps when his supercharger disintegrated. *Below* (BRDC): Gordon Watson's Alta heading for Woodcote during the rain-soaked International Trophy. Geoffrey Taylor's little Kingston-upon-Thames firm of Alta primarily built road cars. Their F1 endeavour of 1950–52 brought good publicity but limited results.

Amateur and Professional

Dublin motor trader and property dealer Joe Kelly, thirty-seven, negotiating Stowe in the 1950 GP in his own dark-green Alta. *Below*: Forty-four-year-old Louis Rosier, owner of a major Renault dealership at Clermont-Ferrand and boss of the highly professional 'Ecurie Rosier', en route to fifth place in his Lago-Talbot. Rosier, closer to the straw bales than Kelly at the same corner's apex and much more intense, was to perish after crashing at Montlhéry in 1956. Kelly died a very rich man, at eighty.

Winners and Losers

Farina being congratulated by the *Daily Express'* Max Aitken after winning the 1950 International Trophy. *Below*: The accomplished French driver Raymond Sommer at the same International Trophy meeting, about to suffer the great embarrassment of BRM's much-derided start line breakdown. Tragically, the forty-four-year-old Sommer was to lose his life only a month later, when racing his own car in France. Like Louis Rosier, he had risked his life in brave exploits in the French Resistance during the war. (Photos: BRDC)

Ferrari v Alfa Romeo

Above (BRDC): Competitors gathering for the Grand Prix of 1951. Farina studies his Alfa, Ascari his Ferrari 375. The Alfas of Bonetto (4) and Sanesi (3) occupy the second row with Villoresi's Ferrari. At the very back of the grid, enthusiasts swarm around the two 16-cylinder BRMs (Walker and Parnell), neither of which had been able to practise. In the far distance, beyond the flat fields, proudly stood two grandstands at Stowe. *Below:* Peter Walker (7) and Reg Parnell (6) in their BRMs.

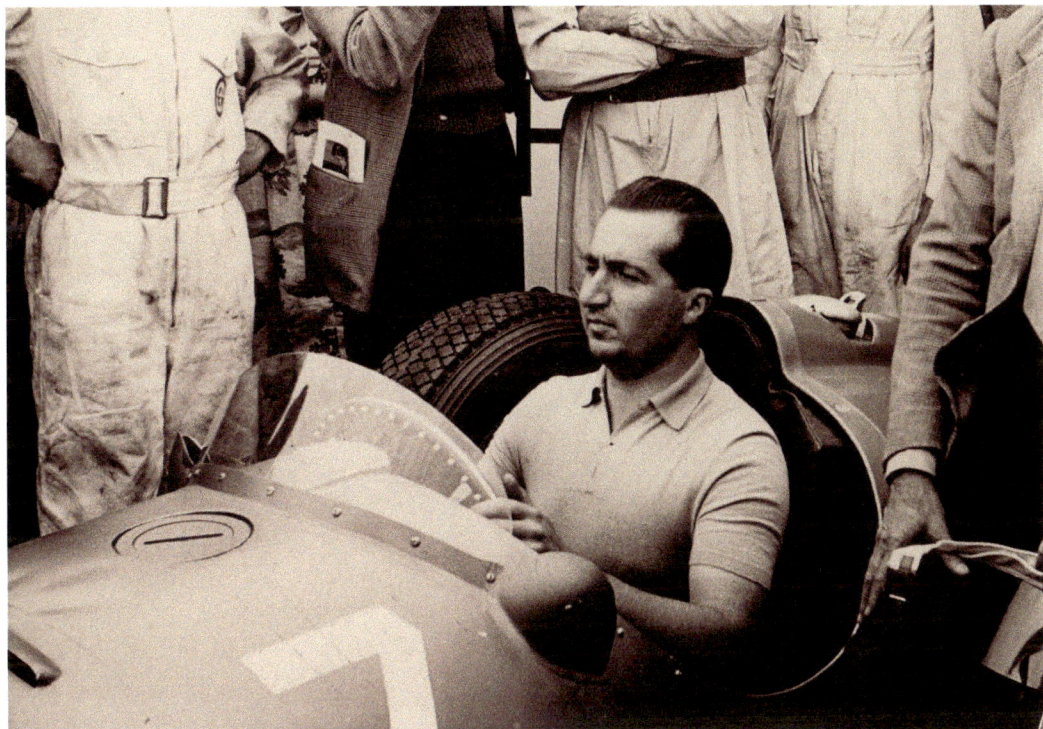

BRM's Glimmer of Hope

A token of BRM's mounting respectability: Ferrari's Alberto Ascari (World Champion in 1952 and 1953) tries Peter Walker's cockpit for size during the Grand Prix meeting of 1951. *Below*: Peter Walker gets away last. By the end of the first lap, however, he was on Parnell's tail. By then they had overtaken the most elderly cars and were lying tenth and eleventh in a field of twenty-one. Both cars were to complete the ninety-lap course, in fifth and seventh, though several laps adrift from the Ferraris and Alfas.

1951: Ferrari's Historic First Grand Prix Victory

The eventual winner, thirty-eight-year-old Argentinian José Gonzales, leads teammate Alberto Ascari (one of the younger drivers, just turned thirty-three) through the Woodcote exit during an early practice session. A grandstand awaits its final touches. *Below* (BRDC): Similarly during practice, the two Alfas of forty-eight-year-old Felice Bonetto (alas, to be killed two years later) and Farina lead Ascari through Stowe. Bonetto, Gonzales and Fangio would all lead the GP on lap one. Gonzales would go on to make Ferrari history.

3

THE FRONT-ENGINED FINALE
1952-59

The 1952 season saw many big changes. For the first time, drivers had to wear helmets (albeit ones originally designed for polo players). Meanwhile, the cars for 1952–53 were restricted to F2 regulations to ensure more competitive fields – bad news for Alfa Romeo, but good news for Ferrari with their attractive Tipo 500. Silverstone, too, changed in a big way. The previous year the British Racing Drivers' Club had taken over its lease from the RAC and determined to create a more permanent facility. The old headquarters area by the farm (pits, paddock, start line and grandstand) were swept away. In their stead, a new start line and headquarters complex was created on the immediate exit from Woodcote, where there was much more room for future development. It was all very propitious. From 1954 the FIA decreed that there were to be engines of 2500 cc, or 1500 with a supercharger. This key change was to underpin the legendary decade that the 1950s became: Formula 1's great front-engined finale.

The new start line area, seen in the GP of 1954, with Stirling Moss (Maserati 250F) and Juan Manuel Fangio (streamlined Mercedes-Benz W196) battling for the lead (which Gonzales' Ferrari would finally inherit). Facilities, however, remained fairly basic. The pits could accommodate the drivers' wives with their lap-charts but little else. The Mercedes team garaged their cars in Brackley, 8 miles away. Other teams used Towcester and Northampton. (BRDC)

Front and Back of the New Pits I
The new pits of 1952, with Ferrari's
three cars to the fore, and, above them,
a delightful observation platform
for spectators with paddock passes.
(Photo: Simon Lewis) In the distance,
the new Woodcote grandstand.
Below: The charmingly rural paddock
at the back of the new pits a year later,
as the evergreen fifty-two-year-old
Louis Chiron, one of the finest drivers
of the interwar years, heads off in
his not particularly competitive Osca
(built by the Maserati brothers in their
factory outside Bologna, after they had
sold up their Maserati factory).

Front and Back of the New Pits II

Above (BRDC): Jean Behra in his Gordini passes the end of the new pits during the International Trophy of 1953. *Below*: The very basic nature of the new pits can be seen from the paddock scene of 1956, with three enthusiasts sizing up Rudy Hernando Ramos' F1 Gordini. The cars of the Italian-born and Paris-based Amedeo 'Amédée' Gordini, who had tuned and raced cars since the 1930s, appeared in F1 in 1950–56. Alas, his beautifully built new engine of 1954 proved underpowered. Gordini eventually became part of Renault.

The Ferrari 500, 1952–53

Farina in the beautiful Ferrari 500 that dominated F1 in 1952–53. Farina himself was to come second in many races to Ascari, but his distinctive upright and straight-armed style was still thrilling spectators (for whom driver visibility was magnificent). *Below*: The veteran Villoresi, before donning his helmet for the 1953 Grand Prix, in which he was to retire. Mike Hawthorn, in only his second season in single-seaters, had joined Villoresi, Ascari and Fangio at Ferrari, impressing with victories at Reims and in the Silverstone International Trophy.

Hawthorn's Fast Vanwall, 1955

The Grand Prix was held at Aintree in 1955 and four foreign teams declined to support the International Trophy that May. Nonetheless, the deep British involvement in F1 ensured a successful event. *Above*: Vanwall mechanics attend Mike Hawthorn's car. *Below*: Hawthorn about to blast into the lead. He shared the front row with the Maseratis of Salvadori and Moss and (out of sight) Jack Fairman's Connaught. Ultimately, Hawthorn retired and Peter Collins won in a Maserati owned (and being carefully studied) by BRM. (Photos: BRDC)

The Pretender and the Champion, 1955–56

Above (BRDC): Peter Collins winning the International Trophy in 1955 in BRM's Maserati 250F. The handsome twenty-three-year-old, son of a garage owner, had six years' racing experience and helpful social skills. His victory with Moss in the Targa Florio that year would get him a Lancia-Ferrari drive. He looked a possible world champion. *Below*: Fangio, world champion in 1951 and 1954–57, chatting to the renowned photographer Louis Klemantaski in 1956. Klemantaski was Collins' passenger in a Ferrari 860 Monza in that year's Mille Miglia.

Mixed Fortunes, 1956

The Grand Prix was at Silverstone in 1956, where corners were now defined by low walls. The Lancia-Ferraris of Fangio and Collins came first and second. (Lancia had retired from F1, handing their cars to Scuderia Ferrari.) *Above*: Alfonso de Portago's Lancia-Ferrari, which Collins took over during the race. *Below*: Tony Brooks' BRM finished its race less successfully, after the throttle stuck open at Abbey. Having run wide on the grass, it somersaulted and ended in flames, upside down. Brooks, fortuitously, had been thrown clear.

Front-engined Ferraris, 1958

The Collins, Hawthorn and von Trips Ferrari 246s on the runway by Woodcote. Their new V6 engines ensured competitiveness and Hawthorn (car 2) had enjoyed a second French Grand Prix victory two weeks before. But it was an unhappy team. Musso had fatally crashed his 246 at Reims. Enzo Ferrari, moreover, had also vainly tried to demote Collins (car 1) from Formula 1, furious that his erstwhile favourite had moved home with his new wife from Maranello to a yacht in Monaco.

Front-engined Finale, 1958

The three Ferraris await the race. *Below*: The Grand Prix start. Peter Collins' Ferrari is behind Moss's Vanwall (7), Salvadori's Cooper (10) and Schell's BRM (20). Cliff Allison's tiny Lotus-Climax is fifth. Mike Hawthorn fights for seventh place after a bad start from the front row. Peter Collins went on to win decisively with Hawthorn second, but two weeks later he was to crash fatally at the Nürburgring. His Ferrari was the last front-engined car to win a Grand Prix. (Photos: BRDC)

The Old and the New

Jean Behra in the 1958 GP in the fifth-placed BRM, one of several makes still enjoying front-engined success. Vanwall, for example, was the leading constructor and it was in a front-engined Ferrari that Hawthorn became world champion. The rear-engined Cooper and Lotus, however, had been leading a revolution that would now change F1. *Below*: Tony Brooks at the 1958 International Trophy in a Cooper-Climax (T45), a successful Owen Maddock design with input from Jack Brabham and John Cooper. (Photos: BRDC)

4

CLARK'S DARK GOLDEN AGE
1960-68

Jack Brabham clinched the rear-engined revolution by winning the world championship of 1959 in a Cooper T51, his victories including the British GP (at Aintree). In 1960, in a Cooper T53 he won the British Grand Prix again (this time at Silverstone) as he went on to a second successive world championship.

In 1961 engines were dramatically reduced to just 1500 cc with no supercharging. The racing was fierce, but weight-saving often meant fragility. Jim Clark began to dominate, with Lotus' Colin Chapman the design trendsetter. In 1962 the Lotus 25 boasted a monocoque (a riveted lightweight metal case instead of a tubular space frame). Soon everyone had to have one.

In 1966 came 'the return to power', a dramatic shift to engines of 3 litres. Though the cars continued to become more sophisticated, not so the measures for the drivers' safety. Regular fatalities were still the deeply distressing norm.

The old airfield's buildings are much in evidence at the International Trophy of 1960. There is still minimal protection for the spectators watching at Club (five years since the Le Mans tragedy). Far right: the works Lotus 18 of Alan Stacey (who died at Spa two weeks later). The Ferraris of Phil Hill (25) and Cliff Allison (24) pursue him. Among lapped backmarkers: David Piper (16) in a Lotus 16 and John Brian Naylor (15) in his own creation. A hangar (now the museum) towers in the background to the right.

The Personable Harry Schell, 1960

Harry Schell in a Cooper T51 of the BRP team, sponsored by Yeoman Credit – it was the first fully sponsored Formula 1 team – practising for the International Trophy. Tragically, he was shortly to crash fatally, after drifting wide at Abbey. Born in France but the son of a dynamic American heiress (herself a racing driver of spirit), Schell for many years successfully combined his sport with running a popular bistro in Paris. *Below* (Simon Lewis): Schell (the second from left) joking with Bira in the Silverstone paddock, 1953.

The International Trophy, 1962

Twenty-six-year-old Jim Clark, after two promising seasons with Team Lotus, starred in the Lotus 24 in 1962. Here he leads Richie Ginther (BRM), Bruce McLaren (Cooper), Innes Ireland (Ferrari loaned to BRP) and Graham Hill (BRM) at the start of the International Trophy race, but in a famous photo finish Hill was to snatch victory at the final corner. Hill became World Champion that year, Clark in 1963. Below: Hill at Stowe, about to lap Surrey car dealer John Campbell-Jones' Emeryson, built by Paul Emery. (Photos: BRDC)

Jim Clark, the Nonpareil
Clark in his state-of-the-art helmet. The simple colour schemes of the helmets of the period were helpful identification aids to spectators, as were the large car numbers. With loudspeakers drowned out by engine noise, there were little other means of identification. (Photo: Simon Lewis) *Below*: Clark winning the British GP of 1963 in his Lotus 25, one of seven victories in the year's ten races. 'Unruffled and unchallenged,' wrote one journalist, 'the Berwickshire farmer won with consummate ease, twenty-six seconds ahead of Surtees' Ferrari.'

Early 1960s: Some Basic Circuit Needs

Leaving Copse (with its minimal run-off area) on the first lap of the International Trophy, 1963, New Zealander Bruce McLaren briefly leads from Clark, Hill and Ireland. Clark would win, but McLaren would found McLaren Automotive that year. *Below*: Keith Greene approaches the pits in a Gilby (built at his father's Ongar garage) at the 1962 Trophy race. The vulnerability of those in this area is all too clear. A tragedy during the Grand Prix meeting of 1963 led to the speedy creation of raised pits. (Photos: BRDC)

Brabham and Hill, 1964

A tractor was still a highly appropriate vehicle to pull the winning car and driver (Jack Brabham and his Brabham BT7) on a victory lap around rustic Silverstone after the International Trophy of 1964. It had been Graham Hill (seen below beside his BRM in the charmingly informal paddock) who had led on the last lap, even as late as Abbey, only to be overtaken by Brabham at the high-speed corner of Woodcote in a thrilling photo finish. (Photos: BRDC)

Cornering Coopers, 1965

In practice for the International Trophy, teammates Bruce McLaren (above) and Jochen Rindt (below) drift round Stowe and Club respectively in their attractive but uncompetitive Cooper-Climax T77s. Both had the roll-over bars required by regulations, but, as was often the case at this period, their low height would have rendered them functionally inadequate. The twenty-three-year-old Austrian was in his first season of F1 and still a raw, promising talent. McLaren would leave Cooper in 1966 to drive his own McLaren 2B. (Photos: BRDC)

New Artistry: Jackie Stewart and BRM, 1965

Above: The twenty-five-year-old Scotsman winning his first F1 race, at the International Trophy in his first season of F1. Under great pressure from Surtees' Ferrari, he remained unflustered. Later in 1965, at Monza, he would win his first Grand Prix. The 1500cc BRM P261, with the marque's first fully monocoque chassis, was (in terms of results and championship points) its most successful car. *Below*: Stewart on his victory lap, rounding Stowe, where spectators were now protected by a brick wall fronted by a wattle fence. (Photos: BRDC)

'The Return of Power'

The new 3-litre formula of 1966 meant many constructors had to move on from Coventry-Climax engines. This caused headaches before the Ford Cosworth came along, though the astute Jack Brabham had the Repco engine, and for two years his Brabhams dominated. However, in the International Trophy race of 1967 Mike Parkes took the Ferrari V12 to an encouraging win. *Above*: Parkes leads Stewart's short-lived BRM at Club. *Below*: Later in the race, Brabham fights Siffert's Cooper-Maserati for second place. (Photos: Simon Lewis)

A Talented Privateer: Bob Anderson

Several race day fatalities in the 1960s at Silverstone led to a number of safety improvements, but the death of the accomplished privateer Bob Anderson on 14 August 1967 could have been avoided had a dangerous marshals' post at the Woodcote end of the club straight been re-sited. Tragically, the thirty-six-year-old slid into it when testing his 1964 Brabham BT11 in damp conditions. Though seat harnesses were not mandatory until 1972, Anderson had bought one and intended to fit it ...

Bob Anderson's modest transporter, a blue VW, had graced the F1 paddocks for five seasons.

A Grim-faced International Trophy, 1968

In April 1968 everyone was stunned by the death of Jim Clark, five times the winner of the British Grand Prix. The International Trophy took place just ten days later. In the programme the BRDC's president, Gerald Lascelles, saluted the 'impeccable master of his art'; on the grid a lone piper played a poignant lament. Then racing resumed. McLarens and BRMs led the charge: Denny Hulme, Mike Spence (killed days later), Bruce McLaren and Pedro Rodriguez. *Below*: Chris Amon's Ferrari chasing Bruce McLaren. (Photos: BRDC)

An Acceptance of High Risk

Post-war motor racing was imbued with the wartime acceptance of deaths resulting from a noble cause. Bruce McLaren declared, 'To do something well is so worthwhile that to die trying to do it better cannot be foolhardy.' Graham Hill's smiling pronouncements on various near-disasters followed this philosophy. *Above*: Bruce McLaren and his M7A, 1968. *Below*: Graham Hill, reigning world champion in 1969, explaining a soluble problem to Prince Charles, Lord Mountbatten and the Duke of Kent. (Photos: BRDC)

5

THE STEWART DOMINANCE
1969-73

After three years with BRM, in 1968 Jackie Stewart renewed his links with Ken Tyrrell, his team manager in his all-conquering F3 days. Tyrrell had just gone into F1 with the French Matra team, using Ford Cosworth engines. He had a no-nonsense approach, without frills. 'We changed in the back of a transporter,' remembered Stewart, 'and Nora Tyrrell did the sandwiches.' They must have been good ones. The first Matra year brought Stewart two wins; the second, five and a world championship. For 1970, Tyrrell, still working from a converted barn in his family's Surrey timber business, ran a car for Stewart from the newly started firm of March, before, in 1971, triumphantly turning constructor himself. Fifteen wins and two more world championships resulted. When Jackie Stewart retired, at thirty-four, he was at the very top of his profession.

From the beginning, he had taken the issue of safety seriously. 'When I arrived in Grand Prix racing, so-called precautions and safety measures were diabolical.' So he spoke his mind. 'I would have been a much more popular world champion if I always said what people wanted to hear. I might have been dead, but definitely more popular!' As chairman of the Grand Prix Drivers' Association he went on for much of the 1970s highlighting the many hazards that, with common sense, financial investment and determination, might be ameliorated. He was pilloried for it at the time. It was a brave, much-needed campaign.

Jackie Stewart, British Grand Prix winner, 1969.

1969: The Brief Fad of High Wings

The season began with this fervent new idea. *Above*: In March, McLaren leads Courage's Brabham and Rindt's Lotus from the Brands Hatch paddock at the Race of Champions. Weeks later, the collapse of fragile wing mountings caused Rindt and teammate Hill huge accidents. 'These wings are insanity and should not be allowed!' declared Rindt. 'But to get any wisdom into Colin Chapman's head is impossible!' Common sense swiftly prevailed. *Below* (BRDC): Rindt in his pole-position Lotus, with its lower, safer wing, at Silverstone in July.

Stewart's Grand Prix of 1969

Jackie Stewart's Matra passes Chris Amon and his Ferrari during practice for the 1969 Grand Prix. The crowded nature of the inadequate pits was not to be addressed for another six years. *Below*: Jochen Rindt and Jackie Stewart were the class of the field and locked in magnificent combat for three-quarters of the race, before a mechanical issue put Rindt out of contention. By the end of the eighty-four laps Stewart's Matra-Cosworth had lapped the entire field. (Photos: BRDC)

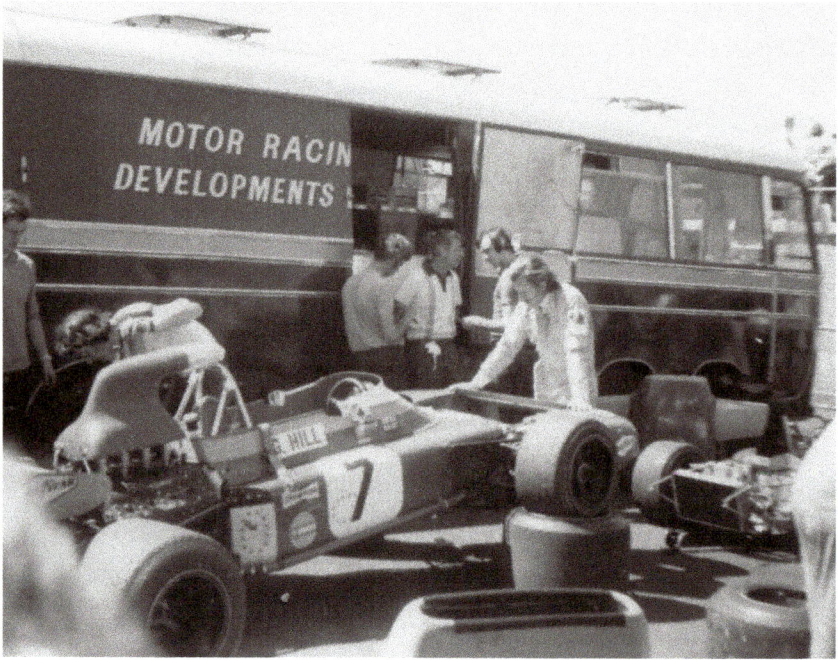

Sombre Reflections, 1971

Graham Hill, in his fourteenth F1 year, musing at the 1971 GP over his 'lobster-claw' Brabham BT34 which was well off the pace. Ironically, two months earlier, in the Trophy race, it had given him what turned out to be his last F1 victory. (Behind, teammate Tim Schenken with Brabham's designer and new owner Ron Tauranac.) *Below*: The popular Jo Siffert en route to qualifying on the Grand Prix front row in his BRM P160, which let him down in the race. Only three months later, at the peak of his career, he lost his life.

The Stewart-Cevert Partnership

Frenchman Francois Cevert supported Jackie Stewart in the Tyrrell team for four seasons (1970–73), coming second in nine Grand Prix and winning once. He was to have led the team in 1974 after Stewart's retirement, but was killed in the last race of 1973, driving 006/3. Stewart is shown above, in 1972, in Tyrrell 005/02; Cevert, below, in Tyrrell 006/01. Many years later, Stewart was delighted to purchase (and drive again) Tyrrell 006/02, the car in which he had won his third world championship.

Revson's McLaren Triumph, 1973

The field of twenty-nine in the British Grand Prix became nineteen after the spectacular high-speed shunt at Woodcote at the end of the first lap, initiated by Jody Scheckter's spinning McLaren. His more seasoned teammate, Peter Revson, is seen on the grid that reconvened an hour later and (below, BRDC) clutching the splendid trophy. It was the talented Revson's first Grand Prix victory. Only nine months later, after one more win with McLaren, a suspension failure on his Shadow DN3 was to result in his tragic death.

6

THE HUNT-LAUDA EPOCH
1973-79

The circuit's biggest changes in this colourful and dramatic epoch came in 1975. First, the Duke of Edinburgh opened a new pits complex at the International Trophy. Then, by the summer's Grand Prix, a Woodcote chicane was in place. Some Silverstone devotees were appalled. Only the year before there had been the great Hunt-Peterson confrontation at this dauntingly fast right-hander. However, the big shunt of 1973 initiated by Scheckter's McLaren had stirred thoughts of cars ending up in the grandstands. Denis Jenkinson might rail against the desecration of Woodcote in *Motor Sport*, but common sense had to prevail. Though comparatively short-lived, the chicane would become an important and even much-liked focal point.

A more disappointing change was the loss in the 1970s of the International Trophy as a Formula 1 race, caused by mounting costs.

Above: James Hunt with the great Mike Hailwood at the International Trophy, 1974. Hailwood, seven years the senior, is said to have taught Hunt how to party. The two were certainly firm friends and kindred spirits. Hunt, however, was always to be remembered for his epic confrontation in 1976 with Niki Lauda. In retrospect, Lauda and Hunt somehow dominate the whole era. Theirs was the classic recipe for drama: the struggle of two great opposites. On the one hand, a supremely dedicated professional; on the other, the inveterate fun-lover, who was briefly having a brave tilt at the professional's dominance. It was a confrontation, too, that was leavened by mutual respect. 'I liked him,' said Lauda. 'We were not buddies, but we were at least simpatico.' (Photo: Simon Lewis)

Great, Late International Trophy Races

Above (BRDC): James Hunt (left) on pole in 1974 in Lord Hesketh's March-Ford. 'Hunt the Shunt' was about to come good. A slipping clutch dropped him to ninth and Peterson's Lotus (centre) led, but Hunt steadily climbed back and overtook Peterson at high speed entering Woodcote to win a famous victory. *Below*: Niki Lauda in 1975 at Copse in the adroit 312T Ferrari, hounded by reigning world champion Emerson Fittipaldi (McLaren M23). After Hunt's retirement when leading, Lauda beat the Brazilian home by just a tenth of a second.

The View from Copse, 1975

Carlos Pace (Brabham) leads Tom Pryce (Shadow) and the Ferraris of Niki Lauda and Clay Regazzoni at the start of the Grand Prix, 1975. *Below*: James Hunt in sixth place heads eventual winner Emerson Fittipaldi. Chaos from torrential rain ended the race on the fifty-sixth of its sixty-seven laps. At least a dozen drivers tangled with the catch fencing, including Pace and Hunt. Note the line of trees in the background, part of what was once the Duke of Buckingham's private road between Stowe House and Silverstone.

A Woman in a Man's World, 1975

Lella Lombardi and Vittorio Brambilla flanked by the bosses of March, Max Mosley and Robin Herd. As usual, Brambilla's March (below) was handling well (and would qualify fifth and come sixth in the Grand Prix) while the talented Lella, only the second woman to compete in Formula 1, as usual struggled with understeer. Brambilla ('the Monza Gorilla') had tried Lella's car and assured Herd it had no problems. Next season, however, after Lella had lost her March works drive, a serious crack in her car's rear bulkhead was discovered ...

A Fast Driver in a Once Fast Car

A thoughtful Ronnie Peterson, sixteenth in qualifying, interviewed in 1975 behind the new pits. *Below*: Peterson struggling during Grand Prix practice, heading for Beckets in the attractive but outdated Lotus 72E ('John Player Special'). Designed by Colin Chapman and Maurice Philippe in 1970, this innovative Lotus had pioneered things like inboard brakes, side-mounted radiators and overhead air intakes. In times past, it had scored twenty Grand Prix wins (seven with Ronnie Peterson). It would win no more.

The Champion and the Pretender, 1975

Niki Lauda, seen behind the Ferrari pit, was in his second season with the Scuderia, on his way to winning his first world championship, though the storm-wrecked Silverstone Grand Prix was to bring him no points. *Below*: James Hunt on a sunny practice day in 'Doc' Postlethwaite's admirable Hesketh 308B in which he came fourth in the world championship. Though the Hesketh bubble was about to burst, Hunt's fine efforts earned him a McLaren drive for 1976, the season of his world championship, immortalised by the film *Rush*.

The Graham Hill International Trophy, 1976

An early Hunt success with McLaren came in the BRDC's commemoration of the great Graham Hill, only four months after his tragic plane crash. *Above*: Serious faces on the ad hoc podium as Hunt prepares to receive the rewards of victory. Below: The atmosphere lightens. Evading action is needed by all the notables (including commentator Peter Scott-Russell, Gerald Lascelles and McLaren's Teddy Meyer). In the background, the wartime hangar and water tower look on somewhat gloomily.

A Continuing Rivalry, 1977

James Hunt at Beckets in the McLaren M26, proudly numbered 1. Though never as good as the M23, it made the front row and Hunt won the race. Niki Lauda, however, clung on to second and won his second world championship. *Below*: Lauda at Copse in first practice in his Ferrari 312T2. Back to his old form after his traumas in 1976, he had had four years of coping with Maranello politics and was about to do the unthinkable: walk out on Enzo Ferrari. He had done a secret deal with Bernie Ecclestone at Brabham ...

A Short but Unfading Pre-eminence

Above: James Hunt behind the pits at the 1975 GP, just before qualifying. *Below* (Simon Lewis): Relaxing with a beer after his British Grand Prix victory, 1977. There would be less fun thereafter. In 1978 the revolutionary 'ground effect' of the Lotus 78 'wing car' would make Hunt's M26E look tame, and the death of Ronnie Peterson (whom Hunt had helped pull out of his burning car at Monza) had been deeply shocking. Early in 1979, after twenty retirements in his last twenty-nine races, he suddenly gave up.

Pironi, Quick and Controversial
Didier Pironi broods in the Tyrrell corner of the paddock, 1979. He had good reason. Though largely a copy of the Lotus 79, his Tyrrell 009 (below, in practice for the Grand Prix) had already ended up in the barriers at Monaco and twice lost a wheel at high speed. He was on the eighth row of the grid and finished tenth. Many more dramas awaited Pironi, not least in 1982, with his falling out with Villeneuve, his own career-ending crash and the consequent loss of the world championship.

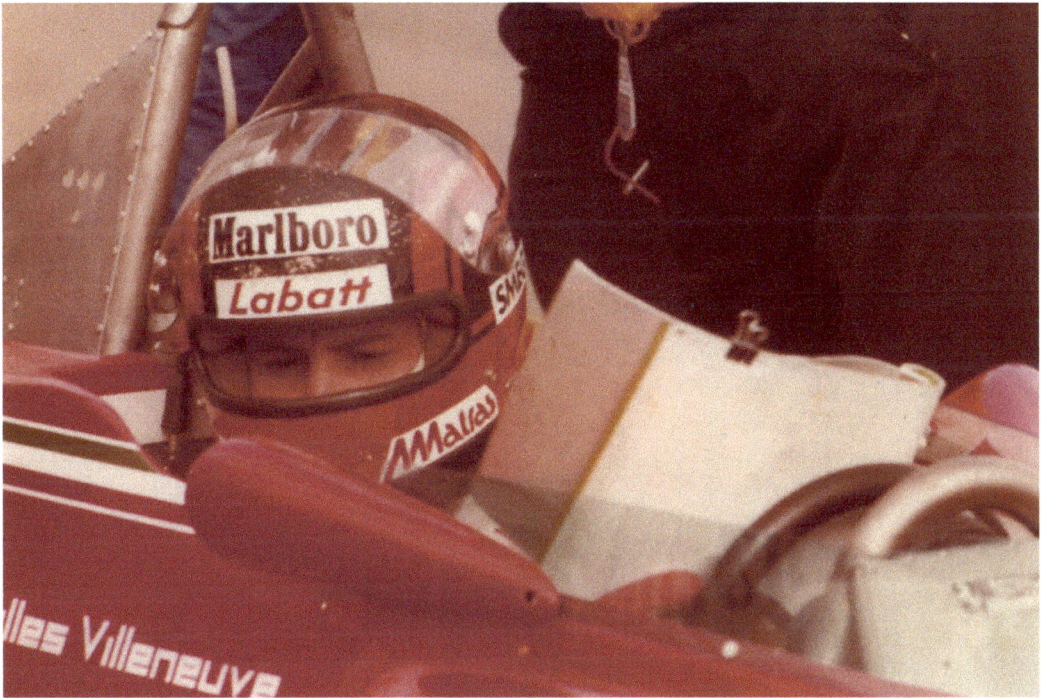

Villeneuve, the Ultimate Crowd-pleaser

The flamboyant and brave Gilles Villeneuve with the Ferrari 312T3 in 1979. He would have become world champion that year had he not obeyed team orders and kept behind Jody Scheckter at Monza. Two years earlier Villeneuve had starred at Silverstone in his first Formula 1 drive and, on the sudden defection of Lauda, Enzo Ferrari had pounced: 'When they presented me with this "piccolo Canadese", this miniscule bundle of nerves, I immediately recognised in him the physique of Nuvolari and said to myself, "Let's give him a try".'

Fluctuating Fortunes in Red, 1979

Jody Scheckter only qualified eleventh and came fifth, but he won the championship title in his Ferrari 312T. He had a sound creed: 'Work harder than anyone else, for that's probably the biggest secret to being successful.' Perhaps this helped him to beat his teammate Villeneuve to the title by four points. He was always shrewd as well as quick. (He is said to have persuaded Enzo Ferrari to sell him his 312T for $80,000.) *Below*: Niki Lauda in the quick but troublesome Brabham-Alfa Romeo. He would be regretting his defection from Maranello.

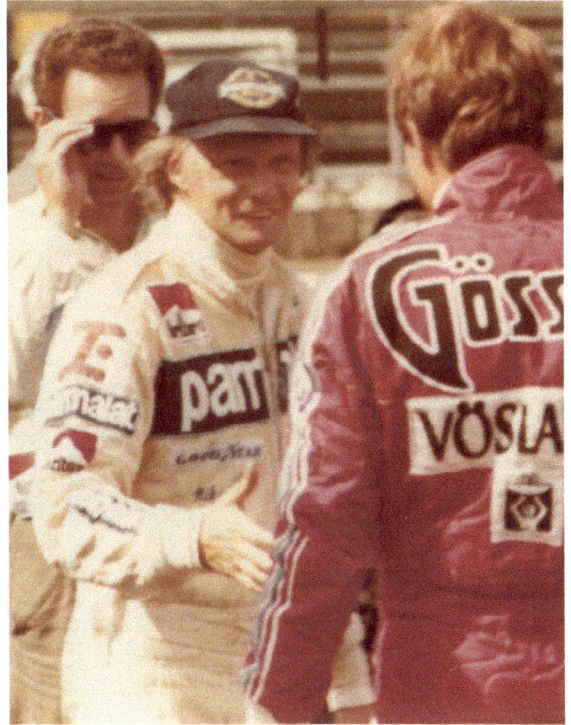

Niki and Nelson, 1979

Top left: Lauda's teammate Nelson Piquet, who managed fourth on the grid to Lauda's sixth (and Lauda usually outdrove all teammates). *Elsewhere*: Lauda meets up with fellow Austrian Dieter Quester (racing a BMW in a supporting event) in the crowded pre-race paddock before the Red Arrows' arrival stops conversation. Lauda had had enough of his Brabham's retirements and would soon be retiring himself. 'I didn't want to drive around in circles any more', he declared famously. In 1982, however, he would return with McLaren.

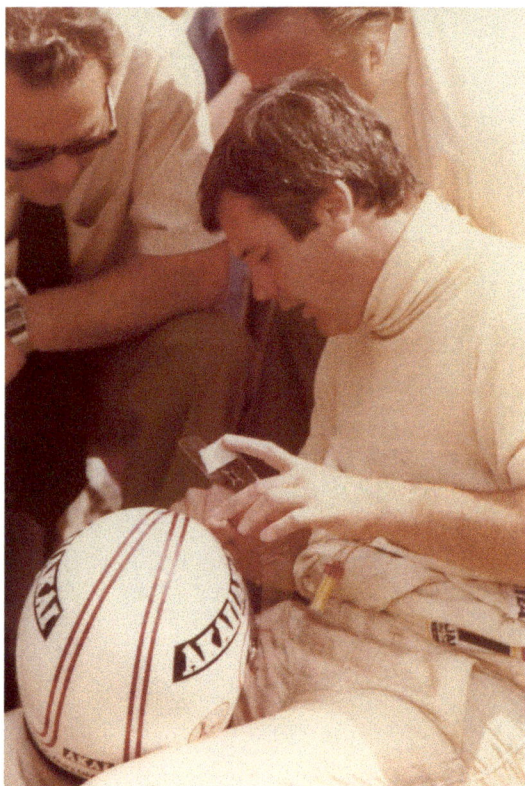

A Memorable Day for Williams

Top left: Alan Jones prepares for the 1979 Grand Prix. He was leading in his Williams FW07 but retired on lap thirty-eight. Instead, victory went to his teammate, the popular Swiss driver Clay Regazzoni (*top right*), giving Frank Williams the first of what would be many Grand Prix victories. *Below*: Jones leads Jean-Pierre Jabouille and Regazzoni into Copse at the start. Jabouille's Renault RS10, with its victory at Dijon, had just become the first turbocharged car to win a Grand Prix. But he would be forced to retire, and would do so time and time again.

7

THREE TITANS: PROST, MANSELL AND SENNA
1981-93

The Formula 1 circus only visited Silverstone four times in the first seven years of the 1980s, but the situation would soon improve. In 1986 the Fédération Internationale du Sport Automobile decreed that each host country's Grand Prix should have just one designated venue, and so, thereafter, Brands Hatch ceased to share the event with Silverstone. The circus' new ringmaster was soon cracking his whip about the facilities on offer: 'Silverstone has undertaken to build a totally new pit complex,' announced Bernie Ecclestone, the Chief Executive of the F1 Constructors' Association, 'and complete long-term improvements which will really make it the centre of British motor racing.' The considerable change that was heroically effected by the BRDC over six years included new pit garages and a media centre. Vale corner was added between Stowe and Club and an S bend replaced the Woodcote chicane. The latter, in turn, was replaced in 1990–91 by a whole 'stadium complex', introduced by a stern right-hander at 'Bridge', shortly after Abbey.

The era of 1981–93 was dominated by Alain Prost, winner of five British Grand Prix. From 1985 he faced major competition from Nigel Mansell and Ayrton Senna. In his eight Silverstone GPs, Senna never qualified lower than fourth. He was always there and abouts. Meanwhile, three of Mansell's thirty-one Grand Prix victories were to come at Silverstone. 'Mansell Mania' developed amidst this clash of Titans.

Ayrton Senna in 1989 leads his McLaren-Honda teammate and arch rival Alain Prost. Senna would spin off and Prost win. (Photo: BRDC)

Turbo-age Problems, 1981

Above (BRDC): Teammates Villeneuve and Pironi test the 126C, Ferrari's first turbo car. Villeneuve likened its massive power and dreadful handling to 'a big red Cadillac'. Though eighth and fourth in Grand Prix qualifying, neither finished the race. *Below* (Simon Lewis): Colin Chapman, without a turbo, hoped his innovative Lotus 88 might help. Instead, it was banned at Silverstone, its 'double monocoque' maximising 'ground effect' but infringing a rule on 'moveable aerodynamic devices'. Bad news for Nigel Mansell who had just joined Lotus.

Our Nigel, 1983

Nigel Mansell in the new Lotus 94T of 1983, the first Lotus with a turbo and the first designed after Chapman's death. The car's late completion had meant Mansell was only eighteenth on the grid (whereas his senior teammate, Elio De Angelis, was fourth). But a storming drive ended with a magnificent fourth place. (*Below*: Mansell has already passed Baldi's Alfa Romeo and Lauda's McLaren on the first lap.) Silverstone had a new local hero. Mansell mania would soon ensue, gathering remarkable momentum as his career unfolded. (Photos: BRDC)

WILLIAMS FW08C

The car was updated for the 1983 Formula One season to become the FW08C. Under new regulations all ground effect was out and flat bottom cars were in, meaning nearly all the cars in Formula One had to be heavily modified or replaced and the FW08 was no different. Against the turbo cars of Renault, Brabham and Ferrari, Williams were not expected to do as well as they did.
Keke Rosberg opened the season with pole position at the Brazilian Grand Prix (the last for a Ford-Cosworth DFV powered car) and scored the car's last win at the 1983 Monaco Grand Prix.
Rosberg would eventually finish in the Drivers' Championship, while Williams finished 1983 in fourth place, the best of the Cosworth-powered cars.

The FW08C was the first Formula One car ever driven by racing Ayrton Senna, at Donington Park in July 1983, after he badge team boss Frank Williams for a test after being sat beside Senna completed 40 laps and lapped the circuit managed in the car, including 1983 Laffite.

Classic Williams Machinery

A 1983 Williams FW08C, powered by a Ford Cosworth engine, on display at Silverstone in 2018. A development of the car with which Keke Rosberg had won the 1982 world championship, it is mainly remembered as the first F1 car that car Ayrton Senna ever drove (on a one-off testing session). His stellar career took off soon after, with Toleman in 1984. *Below* (BRDC): Keke Rosberg with a turbocharged Williams-Honda in 1985. His pole position recorded Silverstone's first lap time averaging over 160 mph.

A Troublesome Tendency of Turbos

The turbos continued to make for speedy and expensive racing but questionable reliability. *Above*: Andrea de Cesaris' Brabham-BMW blows up at Maggots in 1987, a great spectacle for the brave souls perched on top of the hoardings. It was BMW's last season with Brabham. Bernie Ecclestone's too. After fifteen years' ownership, he sold Brabham for over $5 million. *Below*: The magnificent Porsche TAG engine of Stefan Johansson's McLaren gives up at the same race, on the entrance to the pits. The spectators look vulnerable. (Photos: BRDC)

1987: Senna's Yellow Lotus

Above (Simon Lewis): Twenty-seven-year-old Ayrton Senna in his third and last season with Lotus, their tobacco sponsorship having changed from John Player to Camel and their engines from Renault to Honda. Alas for Ayrton – below, in practice for the Grand Prix (BRDC) – Williams had the latest Honda engine and Lotus the previous year's version. He was third in both the race and qualifying, only headed by Mansell and Piquet's Williams. Senna's exploits in the Lotus 99T would bring him a McLaren drive in 1988 as Prost's teammate.

Performance Imparity

Alex Caffi's new Osella-Alfa Romeo exiting the new S bend ('Luffield'), 1987. Twentieth on the grid of twenty-five, the Osella retired, as it would from twelve other Grand Prix that year. An admirable driver, Caffi could not perform miracles. *Below*: Ayrton Senna's Lotus in the middle of the same new feature during practice. The glitz of the F1 circus with its succession of star performers has always had to compensate for one inherent weakness: significant performance imparity. (Photos: BRDC)

Mansell and Piquet, Williams Teammates, 1987

Mansell (above) and Piquet (below) approaching Woodcote in practice. Piquet ended up on pole but Mansell hounded him until, on lap thirty-five, dropping 28 seconds behind after an unscheduled pit stop. 'I settled into a rhythm and found myself catching him by almost a second a lap!' The crowd roared him on. 'It was like a flipping Mexican wave all the way around the circuit. Just incredible!' After breaking the lap record, time and time again, Mansell passed Piquet on the entrance to Stowe, three laps from the end. (Photos: BRDC)

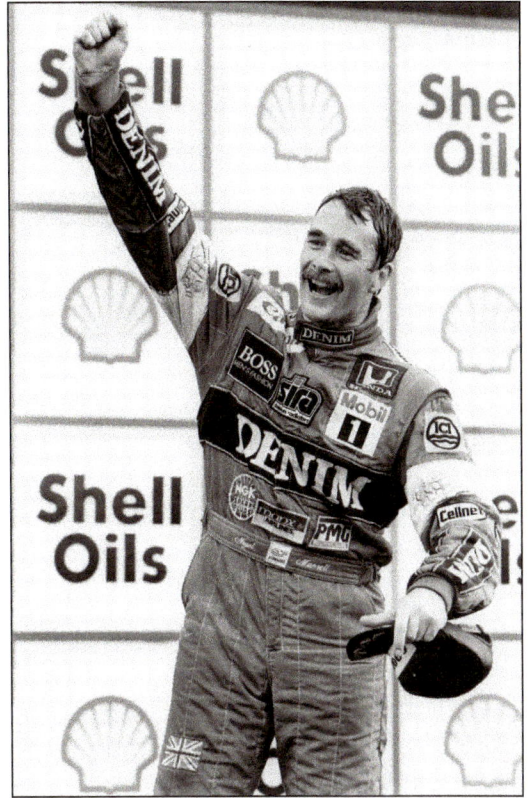

The Joy of Success, 1987

Nigel Mansell would later say, 'I knew I had to sell Nelson a dummy. I knew I had to get his head to turn in the cockpit. As soon as I had managed to do that, then I knew I had him. Even then, he came across on me going into Stowe and we touched at 200 mph. In those days you could block and do anything you bloody well wanted!' *Below*: Ayrton Senna winning the 1988 Grand Prix in the McLaren MP4/4, one of his eight victories that year. (Photos: BRDC)

Spurred by Great Rivalry

Alain Prost ('The Professor') in the winning McLaren-Honda of 1989 (BRDC) and, below, during the 1993 meeting, driving a Williams. Senna was leading in 1989 when gearbox trouble led to his spinning off at Beckets early on. The Prost-Senna rivalry was at its most intense in 1988 and 1989, when, as McLaren teammates, they were in the two fastest cars. Though Prost was outscored by Senna on pole positions by 4-26 and victories 11-14, the wily skills of Alain Prost ensured him one of those two world championships.

Mansell and Ferrari

Mansell's two seasons with Ferrari began in 1989 with an immediate victory. The *tifosi* loved his rugged, lion-like style and he soon became *il leone*. Mechanical reliability proved elusive, however, and when Alain Prost arrived in 1990, demoting Mansell to No. 2 status as he himself won his third world title, the British driver decided to return to Williams. *Above* (BRDC): Anxious work in Mansell's pit at the 1990 Grand Prix, which was won by Prost. *Below* (Simon Lewis): Mansell leaving the pit road in his Ferrari 641/2.

A Champion's Car, 1992

On loan in the Interactive Museum from Williams Heritage: the FW14B ('red five') with which Nigel Mansell won the British GP of 1992. After eleven full seasons in Formula 1 in which he had come tantalisingly close to the drivers' title on three occasions, Mansell finally achieved his ambition. The joy at Silverstone was unrestrained as Mansell's Williams outstripped teammate Riccardo Patrese and the rest of the field. It was his seventh victory in the first nine races, and there were two to come in that sixteen-race season of glory.

Pre-race Crowd-pleasing, 1993

Johnny Herbert, who was driving for Lotus, on the back of a Lotus Elan during a crowd-pleasing pre-race tour of the circuit. Although Herbert would come fourth in the race, he was in his second and last full season with Team Lotus, now at the very end of its distinguished career. Below, the popular French driver Jean Alesi, taken round in a Ferrari 166 Barchetta that Villoresi had once driven in the great road race, the *Targa Florio*. Alesi's promise was never realised. He came ninth in this Grand Prix. His thirteen-year Formula 1 career yielded but one victory.

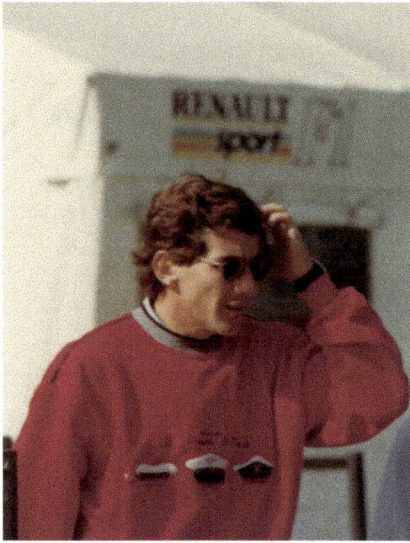

Silverstone Finales, 1993

Ayrton Senna and Alain Prost during what was to be their final British Grand Prix. Prost (below, in his victorious Canon Williams-Renault with the new grandstand at Priory behind) had come back from a year's retirement for a final year, his only one with Williams. It brought him his fourth world championship. 'He can go stunningly fast,' said Williams, 'without looking as if he's trying.' On the Professor's retirement, Senna (above, in the Silverstone paddock, 1993) was to inherit his Williams drive. Tragically, it only lasted three Grand Prix.

8

THE SCHUMACHER ERA
1994-2006

Either side of the new millennium Michael Schumacher dominated Formula1 as no driver had previously done, winning the world championship seven times, twice with Benetton and five times during nine highly fruitful seasons with Ferrari. At Silverstone he did not always enjoy the dominance displayed at some other circuits. His only pole position in this era came in 2001, when he had already won forty poles elsewhere. In 1999, too, a brake failure ended his race with a bad crash and injury at Stowe. But he still won three British Grand Prix (in 1998, 2002 and 2004) and throughout this era it was always the formidable Michael Schumacher who set the most significant benchmark. His partnership with the Ferrari technical director Ross Brawn was truly awesome, particularly in the first five years of the millennium.

Silverstone flourished during the Schumacher dominance. Its steady programme of circuit improvements was hastened by two big wake-up calls at the beginning of the era. Following the Senna tragedy at Imola in 1994, the BRDC initiated £1.5 million of safety modifications to the circuit. Only weeks after Imola, Pedro Lamy's Lotus suffered a breakage in testing, going off the track at 150 mph and ending up in a (mercifully empty) spectator area. A chicane was speedily installed at Abbey.

Michael Schumacher in 1996, his first season with Ferrari. Third on the grid, he would retire with transmission trouble after three laps. (Photo: Simon Lewis)

Doughty Opponents

Above (Simon Lewis): Damon Hill, the Williams team leader after Senna's death, responded strongly in these early seasons of Schumacher dominance. He took pole position in three consecutive British Grand Prix (1994–96) and won the first of these races. Runner-up to Schumacher twice, Hill finally became world champion in 1996. *Below*: Jacques Villeneuve (seen here at Silverstone in 2000) was, like Damon, a Williams driver who lived up to a legendary father. Twice Jacques won the British Grand Prix (1996–97). He also became world champion the latter year.

The Luck of the Draw: Brundle and Hakkinen

Martin Brundle, the highly popular Sky TV pundit, drove for eight teams in his thirteen-year Formula 1 career, but never with a top car. His only year with McLaren (above, in 1994) unluckily coincided with a troublesome Peugeot engine. He missed out on the fine Mercedes engine by one season. His teammate Mika Hakkinen, however, stayed on to win twenty races and two world championships (1998–99). *Below*: Hakkinen, testing for the British GP of 2001 which would bring him his final McLaren-Mercedes victory. (Photos: BRDC)

When Lucky Strikes Belied Their Name

Jacques Villeneuve's BAR 01 during a testing session, August 1999. Half the car advertised Lucky Strike cigarettes and half advertised 555. Alas, the Canadian's bold move to form his own team in 1999, sponsored by the mighty British American Tobacco corporation, only led to several seasons of frustration for the former world champion and Indy 500 winner. But in a sport bound up in regulations and highly conscious of public relations, Villeneuve continued to offer a delightfully outspoken and unpredictable presence.

Testing Testing, 1999

Johnny Herbert testing the F1 Stewart a month after a modest 1999 GP (eleventh in qualification, twelfth in the race). However, Johnny did manage to register that year the solitary win that Jackie Stewart's team enjoyed in their three seasons. Next year Stewart became Jaguar and, in 2005, Jaguar became Red Bull. *Below*: Mika Hakkinen, testing a month after his pole-winning McLaren retired with an errant back wheel in the 1999 GP. This setback enabled his teammate David Coulthard to take the first of his two British Grand Prix victories.

Stars Rising at Different Speeds

Jenson Button, aged twenty-two, in a Renault in 2002. He was already in his third season of Formula 1. From the start Button looked quick and smooth, but it was not to be until his sixth season, in 2006 when with Honda, that he scored his first Grand Prix win. *Below*: Fernando Alonso at twenty-two in 2003, having succeeded Button in the Renault team. With Renault the fast-rising Alonso would win the British Grand Prix in 2005 and by 2006 be a double world champion. (Photos: Simon Lewis)

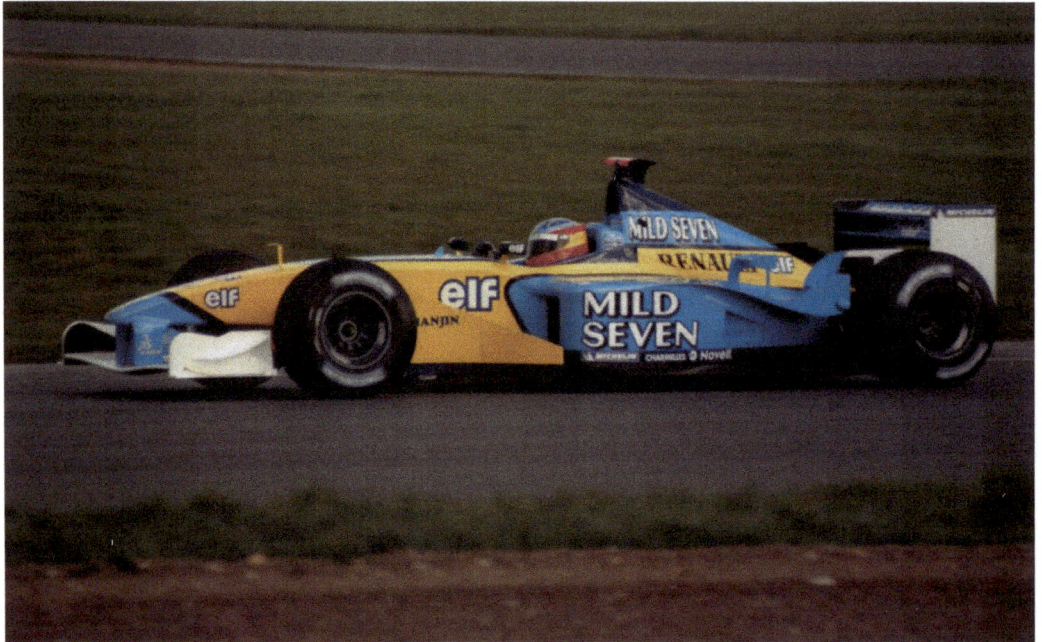

The Quiet Arrival of Red Bull

David Coulthard, seen in 2005, Red Bull's first year as a constructor, when he qualified and finished thirteenth in the Grand Prix. Teammate Christian Klien came fifteenth. The experienced Coulthard proved helpful in leading the team through its first four challenging years. Mark Webber (below, in a Minardi at the 2002 GP) was to be Coulthard's teammate in the last two of them, before starting his long and not always easy relationship with multi-championship winner Sebastian Vettel at Red Bull. (Photos: Simon Lewis)

The Great Michael Schumacher

For all the pace of the Williams initially and the McLarens latterly, Michael Schumacher (above, in the F310B Ferrari in 1997) was pre-eminent. Backing up his flair and ruthlessness was the superb Ferrari boss, Luca di Montezemolo, who 'had learned at the feet of the late Enzo Ferrari and had the same iron will'. *Below*: Rubens Barrichello, Schumacher's long-term teammate, in 2005. Though the great German usually outpaced the Brazilian, at Silverstone Barrichello won the GP of 2003 and outqualified him four times. (Photos: Simon Lewis)

9

NEW HEIGHTS: HAMILTON AND THE WING
2007 ONWARDS

In 2007, a new star appeared. The young Lewis Hamilton looked very special from the beginning, and so it proved. His six years with McLaren brought him one world championship and twenty-one Grand Prix wins. His move to Mercedes began with quiet promise, and then, in 2014, at the start of the hybrid era, when turbocharged V6 engines of 1.6 litres mixed internal combustion with electrification, success followed upon success. In the first seven hybrid years, Lewis Hamilton in his Mercedes won six world championships and six British Grand Prix.

The circuit, too, flourished in this challenging era as never before. Though the cost of staging the Grand Prix was seriously escalating, the BRDC had come under pressure from the company running Formula 1 to invest huge sums in new facilities. Somehow, miraculously, the BRDC steered a course between perilous Scylla and Charybdis. An imaginative re-routing of the circuit between Abbey and Brooklands was effected in 2010. The new pit and paddock complex of The Wing, that architecturally dramatic statement of intent, was ready for the Grand Prix of 2011. How fitting, then, that in 2020, as planning went on for further remarkable additions to the start line area, 'the Hamilton Straight' came into being. For it was in Lewis Hamilton's remarkable era that Silverstone and Formula 1 could at last be said to have jointly become the absolute pinnacle of motor sport.

Hamilton battles for the lead with pole-sitter Verstappen at the start of the 2021 British Grand Prix. He would go on to win the race for the eighth time. (BRDC)

Top Factories, Top Equipment

With its aerodynamic subtleties and controversial double diffuser, Ross Brawn's own F1 Brawn helped Jenson Button to win the 2009 world championship. And Brawn's single year as boss at Brackley had vital future implications, his takeover of Honda's state-of-the-art factory leading to it becoming Mercedes' home in 2010. Meanwhile, at nearby Milton Keynes, Red Bull produced the splendid RB6, with which Vettel just pipped Webber for the world title. *Below*: Filmed for the Interactive Museum, Mark Webber reminisces on it all.

MARK WEBBER
TWO TIME BRITISH GRAND PRIX WINNER

- The 2010 RB6 Red Bull
Formula 1 car is a special car.

The View from Club, 2015

Above: The Wing in all its glory at the Grand Prix of 2015. After the major circuit changes of 2010–11, Club assumed extra significance as the last corner before the finish. The pit lane behind the track adds further interest. *Below*: Kimi Raikkonen's third-row Ferrari approaches the grid. The stands on the far side of the new start line were temporary ones. Ironically, the new start line is only a few hundred yards below where the original one had been in 1948–51, alongside the farm on the Abbey-Woodcote straight.

Red Bull and Mercedes Rivalry

Above: Daniel Ricciardo's Red Bull RB10 on resplendent display in the Interactive Museum. It dates to 2014, the start of the hybrid era. Ricciardo (who had taken over from Mark Webber) did well to win three GPs, for 2014 marked a big swing in the fortunes of Red Bull and Mercedes. In the previous four seasons, Vettel had swept the board for Red Bull. In 2014 and again in 2015, however, Lewis Hamilton won victory after victory for Mercedes. *Below*: Hamilton, yet again victorious in his Mercedes, is cheered at Beckets in 2019.

A Bonus for the Modern Spectator I

Although spectators are further away from the cars than in earlier times, there is now the compensation of screens strategically placed all over the circuit. For those prepared to pay extra, hospitality zones offer extra recreational facilities. *Above*: Valtteri Bottas peers down on 'Club Silverstone' in 2019. *Below*: George Russell, with a few details about his first season with Williams. Entertainment from the screen/stage areas would also be a feature. Live music, indeed, has become a more and more integral part of the Silverstone garden parties.

A Bonus for the Modern Spectator II

On-screen coverage for Silverstone spectators could hardly be bettered. *Above*: In 2019, even early on in the long weekend pre-practice, Johnny Herbert is interviewing the promising new arrival, McLaren's Lando Norris, still only nineteen. *Below*: Ferrari's Charles Leclerc, interviewed after coming a brilliant second that year, splitting the Mercedes of Hamilton and Bottas. (The guitar resting on the screen in the bottom left-hand corner suggests live music will shortly follow at 'Club Silverstone'.)

A Year Before Knighthood

Interviews never stop during a Grand Prix weekend. After the race of 2019, though clearly drained after just achieving his sixth British GP victory and claiming in the process the fastest lap with a new lap record, thirty-four-year-old Lewis Hamilton speaks and listens carefully to post-race interviewer Jenson Button, just below the podium. He is to be knighted next year, the fourth Formula 1 driver (after Jack Brabham, Stirling Moss and Jackie Stewart) to enjoy this distinction, and the only one so honoured while still racing.

2020: Two Races with Empty Stands

Formula 1 came to Silverstone in consecutive weeks during the summer of 2020, when, with the pandemic at its early height, a race celebrating the seventieth anniversary of Formula 1's beginning was also held, a week after the British Grand Prix. Max Verstappen (seen with teammate Sergio Perez) won the anniversary race and came second in the GP. Still only twenty-two at the time, the formidable Max was already in his sixth season of F1 and promising to renew the Red Bull dominance that it had earlier enjoyed with Sebastian Vettel.

Victory Again in 2021

Like most modern sports stars, the Grand Prix drivers are practised interviewees, somehow able to offer a coherent word or two in the most stressful of situations. Lewis Hamilton's skills before a microphone or a large crowd mirror his skills behind the wheel. *Above*: He chats after the Grand Prix with equanimity. *Below*: He diverts off the track on his victory lap to be close to fans. The superb Sky television coverage of the Grand Prix circus has had an enormous impact since the beginning of its dedicated F1 channel in 2012.

The Expansion of the Site

Above: The smart new hotel facing the pits (the Hilton Garden Inn) taking shape in summer 2021. *Below*: The decision to implement the 2010–11 improvement scheme would have meant some heavy loans. Accordingly, the BRDC sold off a large area surrounding the circuit. It meant that the circuit would be fringed with modern factory buildings and have unusual companions like the Silverstone Technical College and perhaps some luxury homes. The atmosphere has certainly changed. It is now as vibrant as Formula 1 itself.

The Interactive Museum

The idea of converting the last remaining wartime hangar into a modern, interactive museum was a masterly one. The lower photograph (which also shows one of the last remaining trees of the Duke of Buckingham's drive) emphasises its sheer size. The museum sets out the whole sweep of Silverstone's history in a wonderfully accessible way that engages all ages, the coverage of the fruitful association with Formula 1 being particularly good. Its splendid teashop and imaginative souvenir shop are also highly recommended!

The hangar which is now the Interactive Museum forms the backdrop to the leading cars (Hill, Senna, Prost and Schumacher) racing between Brooklands and Luffield in 1993. The Interactive Museum has its own entrance just outside the circuit and is open six days a week throughout the year. Tickets can be pre-booked online.

ACKNOWLEDGEMENTS

Huge thanks for all the help from Silverstone and, in particular, from David Freestone, the Collections and Research Officer, Stephanie Sykes-Dugmore, the Head of Collections and Research, and Alison Hill, PR and Communications Consultant. Simon Lewis of the Simon Lewis Transport Bookshop has also been another much-valued source of assistance. Thanks, as ever, to Heather Meredith and Doreen Blackwell, always supportive and enthusiastic. Very many thanks, too, to Amberley's Nick Grant and Jenny Bennett.

Photographs from the BRDC/Archive SHL on pages 2, 11, 12b (below), 14, 15b, 17, 18a (above), 19, 20a, 21, 23a, 25a, 26a, 29, 30, 33, 35–38, 41–43, 44b, 45, 48, 50a, 63, 64a, 65, 66b, 67, 68b, 69–71, 72a, 73a, 78a, 85 and 86. Photographs from Simon Lewis: 22a, 32b, 34a, 39, 49, 57a, 58, 64b, 68a, 72b, 73b, 77, 78a, 79 and 82–84. Photographs from Anthony Meredith: 5–7, 8b, 9b,13, 44a, 46, 47, 51–56, 57b, 58–62, 66a, 72b, 74–76, 78b, 80–81 and 86–96. Photographs from Gordon Blackwell: 8a, 9a, 10, 12a,14a,15a,16, 18b, 20b, 22b, 23b, 24, 25b, 26b, 27 and 28. Every effort has been made to find out and advertise all illustrative sources. Any failures to acknowledge other people's labours or work, despite best intentions, will be rectified in any subsequent editions.